Gc
974.402
So89j
1546647

M. L

GENEALOGY COLLECTION

Gc

OLD QUAKER VILLAGE

South Yarmouth, Massachusetts

No land of beauty art thou, Old Cape,
  But a prouder name we crave,
The home of the purest, bravest hearts,
  That traverse the dark blue wave.
Then cherished for aye shall thy mem'ry be,
  For where'er through life I roam,
My heart will turn, like a wearied bird,
  To my own, my Cape Cod home.
        —E. J. Dudley.

Reminiscences Gathered and Edited by

1915

1546647

Copyright, 1915,
By Charles Warner Swift.

BASS RIVER.

There's a gently flowing river,
  Bordered by whispering trees,
That ebbs and flows in Nobscussett,
  And winds through Mattacheese.

Surely the Indians loved it,
  In the ages so dim and gray,
River beloved of the pale-face,
  Who dwell near its banks today!

They pass on,—the generations—
  Thou stayest, while men depart;
They go with thy lovely changes
  Shrined in each failing heart.

Beautiful old Bass river!
  Girt round with thy murmuring trees;
Long wilt thou flow through Nobscussett,
  And wander through Mattacheese.
              —Arethusa, South Dennis.

BASS RIVER.

At the sound of thy name, what fond mem'ries arise
Of the scenes of my childhood, 'neath soft summer skies!
At each sail on thy surface, or walk on thy shore,
Thy quaint beauty impressed me as never before.

Of the Afton and Tiber the poets have sung;
For the Avon and Danube their harps they have strung.
May the the singer be blest, whosoe'er he may be,
Who shall sing the just praises, dear river, of thee!
                          —Daniel Wing.

The idea of putting upon paper various items of information and interest that might be gathered of South Yarmouth, formerly known as "Quaker Village," was suggested by a former resident of the place who had been greatly interested in a conversation with the late Orlando F. Wood, then one of its oldest residents. Recognizing the fact that our old men are one by one passing away and much interesting and valuable information is being lost, I suggested to Mr. Wood that he describe the village as it was when he was a boy and I would write it down. So, seated in his big chair in the cozy quarters which he liked to designate as the "O. B. S. club," and surrounded by a few congenial listeners and good friends, he took each street and described its appearance at that early period.

I wish to state at this point, however, that I have not relied entirely upon Mr. Wood's account, but have had valuable assistance from Mr. Daniel Wing, who has for years made a study of the history of South Yarmouth.

One is apt to think that these country villages change but little, but he has only to let his mind wander back even so short a time as twenty-five years to see that many changes have taken place, and that the Quaker Village of that period was a far different place than that of today; fifty or seventy-five years have brought about great changes.

There is one thing that I cannot but remark, and that is the "youngness" of the present day residents. Even when I was a boy, a man or woman who had reached the age of fifty years was considered "old;" now, he or she is simply in the prime of life and best able to enjoy it. And still more strange, none of those whom I considered old in my boyhood days ever seemed to grow any older! In those days, a man who had reached the age of fifty no longer thought of mingling with the young in society. It was his duty to set the example of sedateness and propriety, as if it were a sin to grow young in heart as he grew older in years. My father was fifty years old when I was born, and he was considered so old a man that his friends told him he would never live to see me grown up. And yet he did live to see me pass my thirtieth birthday. I remember that he was a much younger man at heart when he was eighty than he was at sixty, and grew far more liberal in his views during the last twenty years of his life. In these days it is rarely we find a man under seventy-five who cares to be thought "old."

Before taking up the appearance of the village, street by street,

as described by Mr. Wood, it would be well to give a bit of the history of South Yarmouth, gathered from various sources, particularly from a series of articles by Mr. Daniel Wing, a former resident, which were published in the Yarmouth Register.

According to Mr. Wing, the town of Yarmouth, in 1713, set off a tract of land "for ye Indian inhabitants to live upon," which included the land from Long pond to Bass river, and from the old Yarmouth road to the lands now owned by Joseph Chase; in fact, what is now the most populous section of the village. The Indians having been killed off by small pox, the town authorized the selectmen in 1778 to sell these lands, reserving a tract for Thomas Greenough, one of the survivors. Greenough afterwards sold more or less of this land, the first of which was to David Kelley, great-grandfather of the present David D. Kelley, in 1790, and was about two acres; on the southwesterly corner of which the structure now known as the "cellar house" was erected.

In 1713, when the town of Yarmouth reserved for the native Indians 160 acres, the Indians, according to Mr. Alden in his "Memorabilia of Yarmouth," equalled the whites in population, but disease thinned their ranks and in 1767 there were but six wigwams inhabited in the whole township. In 1787 but one wigwam was inhabited and that was on the grounds now owned by the Owl club.

Speaking of Indians reminds me that "Nauhaught, the Deacon," the subject of Whittier's poem of that title, lived in South Yarmouth on the south side of Long pond, near the Yarmouth road, and the swamp on the opposite side is today known as "Sarah's swamp," being named for the Deacon's daughter. All are familiar with the story of how he was attacked by several black snakes that began to twine about his legs. One of them reaching his head, Nauhaught opened his mouth, and the snake putting his head inside, the Indian bit it off, whereupon the blood streaming down from the decapitated snake alarmed the rest and they fled. Even to this day traces of an old trail may be seen in the vicinity of Swan pond, where an Indian meeting house once stood. "It is probable," says a writer, "that it was on this path that Nauhaught had his encounter with the snakes." Mr. Alden visited him in his last days and asked him if he was resigned. "Oh yes, Mr. Alden," he replied, "I have always had a pretty good notion of death."

Upon the records of the town of Yarmouth may be found under date of November 17, 1778, "Voted, that the charge made by the

Indians having the small pox, be paid out of the town treasury.

"5th. Then voted that all their effects be sold to pay their charge of having the small pox, and the land formerly belonging to the Indians to live upon be sold or leased.

"6th. Concerning the Indian land—Voted that the town impower the selectmen to lease or sell the Indian land or reserve a piece for Thomas Greenough as they shall think proper."

Some of the Indians of South Yarmouth were first buried on land afterwards owned by Robert Homer, but when it was proposed to use the land for salt works, it so grieved Cato, a negro, whose wife Lucy was an Indian, who occupied the last wigwam in South Yarmouth, that the bodies were disinterred and buried with the others on a hillside near Long pond, which spot is now marked by a monument of boulders bearing the inscription:

"On this slope lie buried
the last native Indians
of Yarmouth."

When the bank back of the monument was dug away for the purpose of making a cranberry bog, several skeletons were found, together with pieces of coffins, showing that the burial place was comparatively modern, although the general idea remains that it was also an ancient burial place as well. Certainly it must have been a part of their old hunting grounds, those old woods, bordering upon the largest pond in the vicinity, which was full of fish and the resort of water fowl, and we can well imagine that it would be an ideal spot for the last resting place of the members of the tribe that once held possession of all these lands.

At the time of Orlando Wood's first recollections, there were but few trees in the village excepting wild cherry trees that bordered the streets, and here and there an apple orchard, evidences of which may now be seen in the yard of Captain Joseph Allen, which trees, although at least one hundred years old, still bear fruit of excellent quality. The cherry trees in front of what is known as the "Katy Kelley house" on Bridge street, I am informed by Seth Kelley, were old trees when his father was a boy, which would be very nearly if not quite a hundred years ago. Trees for ornamentation evidently were thought to be too worldly for those old Friends; to them, there was no place for a tree unless it bore fruit, and the idea of ornamenting streets or grounds with trees was something not to be thought of.

Beginning at Bridge street, Mr. Wood says there was no dwelling beyond it. The "rope-walk" extended to the Friends meeting

house on the main road, but all below it, to the river, was given over to fields and gardens, large portions being used for corn-fields. The present street leading to the David Kelley house was not opened, nor were any of the present houses on that street built. The "toll-house" of course was not built, nor even thought of, and the first house on the street, from the river, was the house in which Mr. Wood was born, on the spot where now stands the paint shop of Manton H. Crowell. The garden of this house was the spot where the bank building now stands. This house was undoubtedly the residence of the first David Kelley, who died in 1816, an enterprising man who bought several acres of the Indian lands. It was a one-story house, with a large unfinished chamber on the second floor, in which were several beds, as was the custom in those days. Mr. Wood remembers that a storm blew out one side of the house and he saw some of the neighborly women standing in the breech admiring the view of the river.

Mr. Wood's father was Zenas Wood and his mother was Mercy Hawes of Yarmouth. He tells a story of his grandmother Lydia, or "Liddy" as she was called, that shows that even in those early days "love laughed at locksmiths." It seems that her parents were strict Quakers, and Liddy, against their objections, had met and fallen in love with a young man of West Barnstable. There was evidently no objection to the young man except that he was not a Friend, and Liddy's parents could not be reconciled to her marrying "out of the meeting." But love will find a way, and when the old folks went to monthly meeting one day, Liddy quietly packed up some of her belongings in a bundle, mounted a horse and rode away to West Barnstable, hiding there in an old grist mill—which was standing up to a few years ago—where the young man met her and took her to the parson's. Her father refused for a long time to forgive her, but the mother finally brought about a reconciliation and Liddy went back to her meeting. This old grist mill was the same that received a grant from the town of Barnstable in 1689 of eight or ten acres at Goodspeed's river and the benefit of the stream forever on condition that the parties interested "should set up a fulling mill on the river and maintain the same for twenty years and full and dress the town's cloth on reasonable terms."— (D. Wing.) The story is told that Aunt Liddy dreamed one night, during her last years, that she saw the vessel on which had sailed a favorite grandson, coming up Boston harbor with the flag at half mast and that the boy was dead. A few days later brought tidings that her dream was but the forerunner of sad news.

I remember, rather vaguely, Zenas Wood as a man of whom the school boys stood in awe, because they imagined that he possessed certain authority and power to arrest them for any misdemeanors of which they might be guilty. I also remember that he had a tall flag pole in his garden and a flag which he used to raise upon patriotic occasions, even as Mr. Wood delighted to do later. Mr. Wood informed me that he, Orlando, was born upon a day of general muster, and that upon that eventful occasion, Uncle George Baker shot off one of his arms by a careless handling of his musket. I can just remember the old man myself. The stump of his arm was a great curiosity to me, and the deft way in which he managed to saw wood, which he used to do for my father. In this old house on Bridge street the late David Kelley lived after he was first married, and later Zeno Baker and others. At the foot of Bridge street was a wharf, to which large vessels were often moored.

The next house on Bridge street was that owned by the late Thomas Collins, then belonging to Abiel Akin, blacksmith, grandfather of the late Peleg P. Akin, who came from New Bedford previous to 1800. He had formerly owned the "cellar house," where the late David K. Akin was born. Previously it was occupied by a potter named Purrington, and the second story was used as a sail-loft. After Abiel built the Collins house and moved into it, the "cellar house" was occupied by one of his children, and during a storm the good woman of the house used to take her children and go to her father's to stay, for fear that the house would blow over! However, the old house has weathered many a storm since those days and still stands as probably one of the most substantial dwellings in the village. Certainly it is one of the most interesting old landmarks of the place. The Collins house was also known as the "Amos Kelley house."

The only other house standing at that time on Bridge street, according to Mr. Wood, was that known as the "Kate Kelley house." It was built by the father of the late David Kelley, and afterwards became the home of his daughter Catherine, of whom the older portion of the community have many pleasant memories.

As has been said, back of these houses, on the right hand side coming from the river, was nothing but open fields excepting upon the road leading to the Friends meeting house, where stood the "rope-walk," which extended from the head of Bridge street to the meeting house grounds. For a description of this old business enterprise I am indebted to the late Stephen Sears and to Mr. Wing,

although Mr. Wood recalled the old building because he worked there when he was a boy. It was built in 1802 by David Kelley the first and Sylvanus Crowell, and the business of making rope was carried on for a number of years,—more than twenty-five at least. At that time there was a large fleet of coasting and fishing vessels that sailed from Bass river, and there was a great demand for the product of the rope-walk. The "walk" was, perhaps, twelve feet wide and seven feet high, with port holes that could be closed by inside shutters. At the north end was the power house, operated by horses to do the heavy work, such as the making of cables and standing rigging. At the opposite or south end was the store house for manufactured goods, etc. Mr. Sears recalled a visit to the place when a lad, and seeing two men and a boy spinning. The men had large wisps of hemp about their waists which they attached to the twisting machine, kept in motion by the boy, and walking with their backs to the machine, paid out the material for some two or three hundred feet, and then returned to the wheel, hanging the newly spun thread to hooks. Mr. Sears thought that the men received two cents a thread for spinning and the boy forty cents a day. The tarring plant was outside the main building. When the business of rope making became no longer profitable, the building was occupied for the making of oil cloth, a man by the name of Jacob Vining being the manager, and Stephen Wing the designer and pattern maker. He (Wing) had always a taste for artistic work of a like nature, which showed itself in the painting of signs, lettering and designing. When this business was given up the structure was taken down and the land gradually sold for building purposes, and on the site of the old rope-walk stand today the dwellings built or occupied by Morris Cole, James F. Kelley, William Haffards, Joseph Crowell, Bartlett White, Charles Farris. Nelson Crowell, the dry goods store of E. D. Kelley and the grocery store of David D. Kelley. In those early days the rope-walk was a convenient passageway to the meeting house in stormy weather and as the owners were themselves Friends, they allowed the worshippers to pass through it, a favor I fear no one of the present day would offer if the building still stood and was owned by other parties.

In looking back to those days I am struck with the fact that there were many opportunities offered to keep the young men at work and at home. The Quakers were not a sea-going people as a rule, but they were full of business ideas and promoters

of many industries. In addition to rope making, there was the salt industry, the fishing business was excellent on our coast, shoe making establishments employed many young men, as did a tailoring shop, a magnesia factory, a tannery, and other opportunities were not wanting; while on the other hand, today there is hardly anything for a young man to do who wishes to live in his native place.

On the opposite side of the road from the rope-walk was a "stretch" of pine woods; tall large trees such as one rarely sees now. These woods extended down to the "flatiron" in front of the house known as the "David Chubbs house."

When the old David Kelley house on Bridge street was torn down a portion of it was used in building that now owned by Frank Crosby, and about the same time the house of Charles Baxter was built, and here he lived and died as did his wife, Aunt Betsey. At present it is occupied by Mrs. Hathaway. Next to it was the house in which Mr. Tripp, one of the earlier school teachers lived, now occupied by Mrs. Crowell, the mother of our postmaster, who at this date is ninety-four years old, and in excellent health.

And now, while we are in the vicinity, it is well to speak of the Friends meeting house, which was then the principal place of worship, and to within a few years of the birth of Mr. Wood, the only place of worship in South Yarmouth. It was built in 1809. Nearly one hundred years before, the society built a meeting house in what is now South Dennis, on a hill overlooking the river. Dennis then being a part of Yarmouth, the old meeting house was that of the Yarmouth Quakers, and more particularly those of South Yarmouth. All the Quakers from the country round, says Mr. Wing, used to attend services there, those from Harwich coming on what is still known as "Quaker path," while those from the vicinity of "Indian town," now known as "Friends village," came on the road leading by "Dinah's pond" and crossing at the "second narrows" in a boat kept there for the purpose. When the present structure was built the old meeting house was sold and floated down the river to its mouth and converted into a dwelling house. It is now standing and is known as the "Waterman Baker house." Its age of nearly two hundred years makes it an object of interest to all.

In those early days the Friends meeting was largely attended, both sides of the house being filled at every service, on Sundays and Thursdays, for it was considered an inexcusable neglect of

duty not to be present. On Fifth day, or Thursday, the children in the schools were excused for the purpose of attending meeting, and the young men left their work to attend.

It is told of the late David Kelley, that when a young man and working in the rope-walk, one Fifth day he did not attend meeting as usual. There was much whispering and smiling among the others, and it turned out that on that particular day his proposed marriage to Phoebe Dudley was announced. She was a niece of Robert and Daniel Wing, senior, and came from Maine to teach school in South Yarmouth, and it was here he first met her. If I am not mistaken, the last marriage ceremony performed in the old meeting house was that of the oldest daughter of the late Henry G. Crowell. A visitor to the old cemetery is struck with the simplicity and neatness of the enclosure, the care taken of the grounds and graves, and above all with the fact that there all are equal; there are no costly monuments proclaiming to the world the wealth of him who sleeps beneath, no carved eulogies reciting the worldly deeds of the sleeper; only a simple stone with the name and date of birth and death, and each stone is like every other in size; the richest man in the place—when he was living—having no more costly stone than his neighbor who had to toil early and late to support his family. I think there are few more impressive resting places for the dead than this little cemetery of the South Yarmouth Quakers.

My own memories of Quaker meeting are very tender. My father did not belong to the meeting, although he always attended, and in his later years sat upon the second seat facing the congregation, an honor accorded him because of his life-long attendance and because of the great respect with which he was held by the members of that meeting. As a boy, I was required to attend on First day, and I remember well how long that hour of quiet seemed to me, and how the sighing of the pines back of the meeting house would often lull me to an inclination to sleep, and with what interest I watched Uncle David Akin and Aunt Ruth Baker to see if they showed any signs of shaking hands, which was the closing ceremony.

The old meeting house is closed; all the old Friends are sleeping in the little cemetery. Only a few of the younger members of the meeting remain, and they are so few that to hold services could only cause feelings of sadness as they sit there in solemn silence while their minds harken back to the years that are not, and to the faces of those who once filled the seats.

Facing the "gridiron" was the house of David Chubb, a portion of which was the tailor shop of Alexander Hillman, attached to the house now occupied by Frank Collins, of which I shall have more to say later on. The house has been added to from time to time until it reminds one now of the "house of the seven gables," although how many more gables than seven it has I am still at a loss to say. A large barn is near it, and when I was a boy there used to be a stencilled notice facing the door bearing this information:

> "My will is good,
> My word is just,
> I would if I could,
> But I cannot trust."

David Chubb drove the stage coach for many years and was a well-known personage in the vicinity. And speaking of the stage coach, reminds me that within my recollection the stage coaches ran down the Cape from Hyannis on the south side, and from Yarmouth on the north, and I can see them now, lumbering through the village. I used to envy the driver holding the reins of his four horses and snapping his long whip as he dashed around the corner, with almost invariably a boy clinging to the trunk rack, while some less fortunate urchin sang out, "Whip behind!" To me it seemed like a bit of the circus outside the tent. There are men living in the village who can remember going all the way to Boston in the stage coach, a journey which consumed a whole day. Sometimes passengers went by vessel from Yarmouth, a ball on the top of a flag pole on one of the hills, which could be seen from the village, announcing the departure of such a vessel.

Daniel Wing in a recent article to the Register speaks of the great severity of the weather in those days and of hearing older people tell of walking to the roof of the rope-walk upon frozen snow drifts on the way to the schoolhouse, which stood on the left hand side of the road near the village of Georgetown. I remember hearing similar stories of big snow drifts; one of which was near the foot of Bridge street, so high that an arch was cut into it, through which the stage coach passed. Even within my own recollection the winters were much more severe than those of the present time.

Going back to Bridge street, we come to the street that runs past the house of Thomas Collins to that of the late Peleg P. Akin. There was no building opposite the Collins house, nothing but an open field; but on the corner of the next street leading to the river and to the "cellar house," or near the corner, stood the grocery store of Thomas Akin and the postoffice. There were but two mails a week and these came by the way of Yarmouth and were brought over by carrier. Postage was higher in those days and I have in my possession letters, without envelopes, with postage marked twelve and a half cents. Mr. Wing writes me, "I remember very well the Thomas Akin store when it was on the site here described. The stone wall was very much the same as now, except in front of the store it was removed so as to allow of passage under the store piazza and into the basement. I used to think, when a boy, that the incline leading up to the store on the other side, together with the stone wall and the stairs, was a very grand combination and looked upon it with greater wonderment than I experience now in viewing structures twenty times as high."

Next to Thomas Akin's store, this side of it I think, nearer the corner, was David Akin's jewelry store, one part of which was used by Alexander Hillman as a tailor's shop until he moved across the street to the house now occupied by Frank Collins. Later this little building of David Akin's was moved to Bridge street and used as a postoffice. It is now the dwelling house of Uriah Sears. Thomas Akin was succeeded as postmaster by David Akin, who in turn gave way to John Larkin. Peleg P. Akin was postmaster when the postoffice was in the grocery store, now used as a library room, and he in turn gave place to Bernard L. Baker, who held the office for many years. In the meanwhile, however, the little building had become the postoffice again and continued so until the appointment of the present postmaster, J. W. Crowell, who moved into new quarters.

Down this street, leading to the "cellar house," at the wharf, was the blacksmith shop of Charles and Timothy Akin, the village blacksmiths.

"Uncle Timothy," said Mr. Wood, "was a very keen and witty old Quaker, and very fond of a joke. One day he came to my grandmother's house and said, 'Liddy, I want thee to get thy potatoes and dumplings all ready tomorrow and I will bring thee a goose.' My grandmother thanked him for his kindness, and the next day Uncle Timothy appeared and said, 'Liddy, here is thy goose; it is rather tough and will need a deal of cooking.' And

he pulled out from under his coat a tailor's iron goose! I don't know what my grandmother said, but she kept the goose and it was in the family for many years."

Uncle Timothy was a practical joker and many were the pranks he played upon one and another of the villagers. Althongh some of his jokes resulted in a sacrifice of material, he was always ready to make good the loss, and seemed to count himself the gainer though the fun cost him several hours of labor. "On a certain occasion he partly filled a gun barrel with water, securely closing the muzzle and inserting a plug in the tube so slightly as to allow of its removal by a slight pressure from within. One day Uncle Robert, a boat builder and intimate friend and frequent visitor of Uncle Timothy, called at the smithy and entertained himself, while engaged in conversation, by blowing the huge bellows at the forge. Just then it occurred to the smith that it was a favorable opportunity to try that gun barrel, so, with other irons, he carefully laid it on the fire, and going out of the shop he took a position where he could watch the development of events within; Uncle Robert, meanwhile, ignorant of the preparations, blowing away as if great results depended upon his diligence. As the heat increased, the water in the gun barrel began to boil and the pressure of steam became so great that the plug was forced from the tube, and the issuing steam, after the manner of Hero's engine, caused the gun barrel to leave the fire, sending it in the air in so zig-zag a course as to defy all attempts at predicting where or when it would finally alight. Uncle Robert, who was somewhat corpulent, was entirely taken by surprise, and not knowing what the infernal machine might do next in its mad career about the shop, crawled under the bellows to get out of the way, in which awkward position he was found by the blacksmith, who just then happened(?) to come in to see what on earth was to pay!" (Cape Cod News, 1887.)

Across the street from Thomas Akin's store was the house of Alexander Hillman, (now occupied by Frank Collins) and attached to it was his tailor's shop in which he employed a dozen or more women and boys, the latter being apprentices who were learning the trade, among them being Mr. Wood. Asking Mr. Wood who worked there at that time, I found that many of the women I knew as wives of prominent men in the village were among the number, and others came from Yarmouth, Dennis and Brewster. Evidently some of them were not satisfied with their boarding

places, as the following prayers were written by two of the tailoresses, who possessed a streak of humor in their make-up:

"Lord of love, look down from above
And pity us poor creatures;
Give us some meat that is fit to eat,
And take away the fish and potatoes!"

"Lord make us able
To eat all that is on the table,
Except the dish cloth and ladle!"

Alexander Hillman afterwards removed to New Bedford, where he continued the tailoring business.

Next to this house was that of Cyrenus Kelley, grandfather of William R. Farris, a former resident of this place. It later on became the property of William White, and is now occupied by his son, Edwin M. White. Cyrenus Kelley was a carpenter by trade, and had a shop back of his house. William White was one of a large family that descended in direct line from Peregrine White, the first white child born in New England, and one of the sons, I think Captain Osborn White, has in his possession the cane that belonged to the said Peregrine. William White's direct line from the "Mayflower" is as follows:

1 William White with his wife Anna came over in the Mayflower.
2 Peregrine, first white child born in New England.
3 Jonathan White.
4 Joseph White.
5 Deacon Joseph White.
6 Peregrine.
7 Alfred, William, Perry, Rufus, etc.

On the opposite side of the street was the house of Zeno Kelley, now occupied by Mr. G. W. Tupper. Mr. Wood remembers Uncle Zeno very well because he gave him five dollars a year to milk his cow, and he remembers that one night he forgot to milk. How little things remain in our memories— things that happened long years ago— while events of yesterday are even now forgotten! Uncle Zeno also built and occupied for awhile the house opposite, known as the "Edward Gifford house," one of the most picturesque old houses in the village. He conveyed the premises, says Mr. Wing, in 1805, so that the building is somewhat over a hundred

years old. Uncle Zeno also built the house formerly used as a Methodist parsonage, standing opposite the church on Main street, but which when erected occupied the present site of the late Mrs. Sarah Bray residence.

Uncle Edward Gifford had a large family. One of them—his daughter Sarah R.— I remember quite distinctly as the village dressmaker; a very bright and witty old maid and a great favorite with all who knew her. I recall that at one time, I think it was during the Civil war, she had company to tea and her mother, a hospitable old Quaker lady, said to the young women present at the table, "Girls, eat all the butter thee wishes, but I'm dreadful afraid it will hurt thee." And the eating of too much did hurt the pocketbooks of many of our parents during those times when everything was high and money scarce. Mr. Wing has sent me some of the bills received by Wing & Akin in those days for goods from the wholesalers, and from them I find that the consumer must have paid about sixty cents a pound for butter, one dollar a gallon for kerosene oil, thirty-five cents a pound for sugar, and other things in proportion. It is a wonder that our fathers were able to live and bring up large families of children. Evidently they were living the "simple life."

The street to the water from Edward Gifford's was then a private way and led to the ferry landing which was near the cooper shop of Frederick P. Baker. This cooper shop was built about seventy years ago and was at one time the scene of great industry. One of the sights of my boyhood days was to watch the cooper as he fashioned his barrels, which seemed more wonderful in the various stages than most anything within my experience. I look back to my recollections of Mr. Baker with a great deal of pleasure. He was always one of the most cordial in greeting me when I came home on my vacations from the city, and I recall many a pleasant chat with him in those days when it meant so much to a boy to be noticed by an older man.

The charter for the ferry was granted to David Kelley, and the boats later on were run by "Uncle" Elihu Kelley, who lived on the opposite side of the river. The rates were two cents for a single passenger and twenty-five cents for horse and carriage, which were taken across the stream in a flat bottom boat. "He had a skiff for passengers and a scow for teams," said Mr. Wood, "and a conch shell was tied to a post at the landing, which was blown when the services of the ferryman were needed. The mischievous boys would

often blow the conch to get the old man out." Mr. Wing has this to say of Uncle Elihu:

"Although Uncle Elihu's accustomed place in the Friend's meeting, which he regularly attended though not a member, was upon the 'rising seats,' he was evidently averse to talking much of his religious views, for it is related of him that, when questioned upon that subject by a travelling preacher while the ferry boat was in mid-stream, the old man pretended to be very hard of hearing and replied as he poled the boat vigorously, 'Yes, about half way across;' and upon a repetition of the inquiry, he said, 'Yes, yes, about half way across, half way across,' and so evaded the question."

He was very much opposed to the building of a bridge, declaring that he could see no sense or reason in such a thing; but the bridge was built and the old ferryman's occupation was gone. The bridge was built in 1832, and as the old man lived until October, 1841, he had many chances to cross it if he so wished. Mr. Wing further says, "The several roads leading from the main highway to the river had been but private ways, but even the one leading to the ferry had a gate across the upper end, upon which Tom Lloyd, the schoolmaster, had painted the words, 'To the Ferry,' but the establishment of a bridge necessitated the laying out of a public way, and to this need the Bridge street of today doubtless owes its origin."

As I have said, the bridge was built in 1832, and the late Peleg P. Akin told me that he was the first to cross it, being carried in the arms of his nurse across a planking. Mr. Wing, in one of his Register articles, gives an interesting account of the old tollhouse and also of the present building, which I copy in full, as probably no better account could be written.

"Relegated to a position in the back yard near the river's edge, the original toll-house connected with the Bass river lower bridge now serves as a general storehouse. Its successor, moved a little back from the site occupied by it previous to the time when by action of the state legislature the bridge was made free, is a more pretentious building, which furnished a residence for the tollkeeper. It formerly had an extension of the roof over the side walk. Upon this projecting roof was a large sign giving the rates of toll for all possible combinations of vehicles, passengers and quadrupeds. The first toll-keeper whom I remember was Micajah Baker, who also served in later years as telegraph operator. The toll-house was a favorite resort evenings for men and boys. On

three sides of the room were wooden benches which were generally filled, while Mr. Baker occupied a chair tipped back, in the part of the room farthest from the outer door. A stone water pitcher always stood upon the shelf close by, which was exceedingly popular, especially when the tobacco smoke was thicker than usual; Mr. Baker used to declare that boys walked all the way from Provincetown to drink out of that pitcher. The writer well remembers one evening when the pitcher seemed to be neglected more than usual; but the cause was apparent when it was learned that there was no water in it. After a time a schoolmate volunteered to fill it. He took the pitcher, was gone about the usual length of time, returned and set it in its accustomed place. The first one who sampled the contents, made a wry face, quite perceptible to the knowing ones, but said nothing and resumed his seat. The explosion came when the second person stepped forward, and then the fact developed that the pitcher had been filled with salt water from the river. The joke was greatly appreciated, but that boy wasn't asked for a long time to fill the pitcher again. Occasionally, during the long winter evenings, the shrewd boy trader having molasses candy and cornballs for sale came in, and trade in that line was generally lively for a time. As the hour for the coming of the evening mail drew near, the attendance in the room gradually diminished, and when word came of its actual arrival, there was a general rush for the postoffice. David Smith, a Mr. Cahoon and another person whose name I do not now recall served as toll keepers after Mr. Baker."

Of course the river has always entered largely in the life of the village, but even this has changed in the course of years. Bass, which were once plentiful in the river, have long since passed it by, and within my recollection one could catch quantities of bluefish with a hook and line from the banks at the mouth of the river. Clams, quahaugs and oysters were once to be had in return for a little labor; now even the clam is found in small numbers, while the other two are almost strangers. The "oldest inhabitant" can remember when the river was almost devoid of eel-grass that makes it now so shallow, while the salt marshes were not in evidence to a great extent, the shores being clear white sand.

On the street leading to the ferry lived Captain Benjamin Tripp, and his son, Joseph Tripp, lived in one half of the house or in the ell. Captain Tripp commanded the schooner "Polly" and was in the lumber business.

The street beginning at the residence of the late Peleg P. Akin, now owned by his daughter, Mrs. G. W. Tupper, and continuing down to what is known as the "magnesia factory street," was then merely a passage way and was called "Cat alley." On one side was Uncle Zeno's apple orchard, and below the Edward Gifford house were salt works as far as what is now called the "red house," and on the shore were two salt mills, one owned by Edward Gifford and the other by Prince Gifford, his brother.

The Lewis Crowell house came next. The "red house," also known as the "witch house," was built, says Mr. Wing, by Joseph Crandon, generally known as "Old Cran," and sold afterwards to Samuel Farris, great-grandfather of William R. Farris. Captain Isaiah Crowell bought the place in 1808 with a strip of land extending from the river to Main street, the northwesterly portion of which is now owned by the Owl club, the building now their headquarters having been erected in 1827.

An interesting story is told of the porch of the "red house." It seems that in 1812 the owner desired to build a porch as an addition to his house, and sent to New Brunswick for the lumber. When the vessel bringing the lumber reached Chatham it was pursued by a British privateer. The captain ran his vessel ashore and he and his crew escaped in boats. The privateersmen, seeing that the cargo was only lumber, sailed away, having first, however, set fire to the vessel. The captain and crew of the burning vessel, seeing the enemy disappear, returned to it, put out the fire, floated the craft and proceeded on the voyage, delivering the cargo in due time. Some of the timbers were charred, but were used and may be seen to this day if one is inquisitive; at least they were seen by the men who were working upon the house a few years ago. Lewis Crowell lived in this house until he died, and after him, his son, Captain Hatsel Crowell, who was lost at sea. Hatsel had three children; the oldest became a sailor and disappeared, no one ever knowing his fate; the other two grew up and both died of consumption. Since that time the house has had many occupants but at present is the summer residence of Charles D. Voorhis.

Mr. Wood says he well remembers when the Isaiah Crowell house was built, (1839) as he and another boy were sent to Dennis to inform the Friends that there would be a "raising" in the morning and a Friends meeting in the afternoon. It was Isaiah Crowell's grandchild who was the last person to be married in the meeting house. He was captain of a ship in early life, and in the

war of 1812 his vessel was captured off St. Johns, Newfoundland, by a British cruiser. He had made several successful voyages previously, which had brought him in a large amount of money, so that, for the days and the place, he was considered a wealthy man. He was for thirty-seven years director of the Yarmouth National bank, and for eighteen years its president. His son, Henry G. Crowell, lived at the old homestead for many years. He was a successful business man in Boston and held many positions of trust under both state and city governments.

Coming back now to the street that runs past the front of the Peleg P. Akin house to Main street, we find that the spot now occupied by the dwelling of Captain Joseph Allen was Uncle Zeno Kelley's apple orchard, and the space was filled with trees, which, as a lady who well remembers them said, were full of pink and white blossoms in the spring time, and she never passes the spot but she seems to see them and smell their fragrance, as she did in the days of long ago. As I have said before, these trees, or those that remain, though very old, still give forth fruit in their season.

Pointing out the house now occupied by C. F. Purrington, Mr. Wood said that when he was a boy it was owned and occupied by Robert Wing, a boat builder. His shop is now Mr. Purrington's woodshed. "The land was bought of David Kelley, senior, in 1810. The frame of the building was originally intended to be erected on the old ferry road in West Dennis." (D. W.) His barn then stood near Main street, nearly opposite the town pump, and was moved to its present location by Mr. Fearing, who owned the place later on. He was a large, stout man of rather genial disposition, I believe. He had a fine garden and grapery in which he took much pride. A man told me that when he was a boy, Uncle Robert hired him to take away a pile of stones from one end of his garden and place them at another spot, and when he had finished the work to the old man's satisfaction, he told him to take them back and place them where he found them; this was his way of helping a boy to earn a little spending money. The house remained in the Wing family for many years, and was at one time the home of Franklin Fearing, who married Maria Wing, a sister of Stephen and Daniel Wing. Mr. Fearing was the proprietor of the magnesia factory, of which I shall have more to say later on. He was a man of more than ordinary education for this section in those days; a man of great intelligence; a man of genial dis-

position, kind-hearted and a thorough gentleman. He served as a member of the school board for many years.

Opposite the Robert Wing house and next to the orchard was the pump and block shop of Prince Gifford, which was afterwards made over into a dwelling house in which Captain Jonathan Sears lived, and later on Bernard L. Baker, for many years the village postmaster. Prince Gifford was a very stern and austere Quaker with—as was not uncommon with the Friends in those days—but little sympathy for other religious beliefs than his own. It was this rigidness that was, in my opinion, the main reason why the Friends have gradually lost their footing in this country; it did not appeal to the young, and when the religious world became more liberal the Friends found it hard to give way. It is true that they too have grown more liberal, that the Friends do not insist upon the strict observances and penalties of years ago, but the change came too late. And yet after all, to me there are no sweeter memories than those of the old Friends and of their meetings. When Prince Gifford built his shop, he insisted that it should be built close to the line of the orchard and of the sidewalk, and so it was built, as may be seen today. The house next to the shop was built by Uncle Zeno, who lived there for awhile, but it afterwards became the property of Prince Gifford and his children still occupy it.

Next to this house was a little country store kept by Silas Baker and later still by his brother, Braddock Baker.

Next to the store and on the corner of Main street was a small house also built by Uncle Zeno. Afterwards it was purchased by the Methodists for a parsonage, although previously it was owned by David Wood, who was the village blacksmith and whose first shop was near the cellar house, but afterwards he used his barn for the purpose. Mr. Wing recalls his business advertisement, which read somewhat as follows:

"Diamonds of the finest water.
Horses shod on scientific principles
at the shop of David Wood."

He moved to New Bedford and was for many years a letter carrier in that city. Previous to its removal, this house was, according to Mr. Wing, occupied by "Jim Hudson," later by Timothy Akin, David K. Akin and his wife Rachel, Doctor Green, and Silas Baker and his wife Ruth H.

Silas Baker piloted the first steamboat that ever sailed into Boston. It was a sort of scow, with no deck, and wood was used for fuel. Coming from the westward and arriving off Bass river, Captain Baker was taken on board as pilot around the Cape. My own recollections of Silas Baker are not very clear, but I remember his wife, Aunt Ruth, who was the principal speaker at the Friends meeting for a great many years. She was a kindly old lady, and at New Years used to have a liberal supply of cornballs and other tempting things for the children who came to wish her a "happy new year." I can remember seeing her walking to Quaker meeting leaning on the arm of Uncle Silas; and I can remember her speaking in meeting and how I used to watch her as she deliberately untied her Quaker bonnet of drab, passed it to the one sitting next to her, and then rising and in a voice of remarkable clearness spoke the words that came to her mind. I remember that she very often had something to say to "my dear young friends." I recall them all now,—Aunt Betsey Akin, Aunt Rhoda Wing, Aunt Tamsen Gifford, and afterwards Aunt Lizzie Stetson,— as they sat upon the "high seats." To me there were never such beautiful women to look upon, excepting my own mother; they always gave me the impression that they indeed communed with God. We have all remarked the beautiful countenances of the Sisters of Charity that we have seen upon the streets; they may not have regular features, they may not possess the physical lines of beauty, but there is something in their faces that makes one think them beautiful; and that was the impression upon my young mind when looking at those older women of the Friends in their quaint but becoming attire. I could not tell you why it was so, but the impression has always remained in my memory.

To the outsider, the men of the Quaker meeting always appeared stern and sedate, but they were by no means free from the spirit of life and enjoyed their jokes and bits of humor as well as anyone. They were just, but sharp in business and generally got the best of a bargain. At the same time, they were full of kindness and hospitality and I think this world, bounded by the limits of South Yarmouth, was better, morally and socially, at that time than it will ever be again.

Before leaving the house of Silas Baker, later the property of Mrs. Sarah Bray, I wish to speak of Aunt Fanny Whelden, a relative of Aunt Ruth's who lived with her many years. Aunt Fanny was what many call a "shouting Methodist," and seemed to enjoy her religion in proportion to the noise she could make in ex-

pressing her feelings. Undoubtedly she was a very excitable woman by nature and found in this way an escapement valve for her pent up feelings. I have sometimes thought that living in a quiet Quaker family was too much for her and that after repressing her emotions for a whole week she let them flow forth at the regular Sunday night prayer meetings. I well remember her as an old woman, going to meeting in winter with her foot stove in one hand and a huge muff and cane or umbrella in the other. She sat in one of the side pews near the pulpit and was always present at prayer meetings, for in those days there were preaching services morning and afternoon and prayer meeting in the evening on the Sabbath. At these latter services Aunt Fanny was in her element and her "amen!" and "bless the Lord!" were interjected at all times. I am sorry to say that those of the younger generation saw much to smile at, and I suppose I was not any better than the other unregenerates, who did not understand that it was simply her way of expressing her joy and happiness. One of her favorite expressions was "Praise be to God!" and one evening while she was speaking some young people, unable to restrain their mirth, left the church, whereupon Aunt Fanny, pointing her finger at them, cried out, "There they go, straight to hell! Praise be to God!"

Going back to "Cat alley" and to the new house built by Isaiah Crowell, we find but three houses on the street leading to Main street, the first being that occupied by the Owl club, which was built in 1827 by Daniel Wing, senior, the father of the present Daniel Wing. The ell of the house has been raised since those days, and the present social hall of the Owl club was formerly a barn. Daniel Wing, senior, was born in East Sandwich in 1800. He was the youngest of ten children of whom four have lived in South Yarmouth, viz.: Rose, wife of Zeno Kelley, Robert, George and Daniel. Daniel came to South Yarmouth in 1823 or 24 and tended salt works. In later years he associated himself with Silas Baker under the firm name of Baker & Wing and was interested in several fishing vessels that fitted out from Bass river. They also carried on the business of general country store in the building between the Prince Gifford house and that of Silas Baker. He was a very popular man in his day and had many friends. He died in 1842.

Mr. Wing gives the following description of the country store spoken of above:

"They dealt in grain and must have had the usual difficulty in

getting back sundry bags loaned to customers, for a notice posted in this store by a young clerk, Joseph Dudley by name, ran as follows:

'No bags to lend; no bags to let;
You need not tease; you need not fret;
You need not twist; you need not wring;
For you'll get no bags from Baker & Wing.'

This clerk, who was quite a mechanical genius, devised a plan for keeping loafers from sitting on the dry goods counter, which was at once original, unique and decidedly effective. Certain needles connected with levers were concealed below the field of action, and the apparatus could be set in motion by a person sitting at a desk near the front window."

Opposite the Daniel Wing house is one now occupied by Frank L. Baker. When Mr. Wood was a boy, Doctor Green, one of the two physicians of the place, lived there, and I am of the impression that he built it. He used to go about the country on horse back, his medicines in his saddle bags, and was a most popular physician and man, I should imagine from what I have been able to learn. The house afterwards came into the possession of Loren Baker and later still into the hands of his son, A. H. Baker, a man of whom those who knew him will always have the kindest of memories.

Between this house and that of David K. Akin, Mr. Wood told me, used to stand the little schoolhouse maintained by the Friends, although previously it stood on the land now occupied by Captain Whittemore (formerly Elisha Taylor's). Among the teachers were H. P. Akin, Rebecca Akin, Mary Davis, Sylvia G. Wing and Elizabeth Sears. I remember the little building when it stood on the road leading to the magnesia factory. It was afterwards taken by Peleg P. Akin and used in the making of additions to his house. I do not know whether there are any photographs of the little building in existence, but it was very small with an entry on the front, and I should imagine could not contain more than twenty-five pupils at the most.

On the corner of the street, facing Pleasant street which runs now to the lower village but at that time only as far as the house of Orlando Baker, stood and still stands the residence of the late David K. Akin, (now the property of Captain Joseph M. Lewis) a staunch old Quaker and a man for those days of wealth and

importance. He was president of the Yarmouth National bank for many years and one who commanded the respect and trust of the community. As his residence was next to that of my father's, I have most vivid recollections of him as a kindly, genial gentleman, who was always a warm friend of all the members of my father's family. I have previously spoken of the little jewelry store that he kept on the street leading to the cellar house, which building is now standing on Bridge street. I have most interesting recollections of a pear tree that stood in his garden, near to the line of my father's fence, which, when I was a boy, was loaded down with tempting fruit, which he liberally gave to me from time to time.

His son, Peleg P. Akin, lived in the Zeno Kelley house on the road leading to the ferry, where he died in January, 1903. The present generation is familiar with his life and it is not necessary for me to insert any eulogies of him in this place. He was a man of a naturally retiring disposition, never coveting honors, and yet never shirking the duties of public trusts thrust upon him. The savings bank of the place owes much to his fidelity and because of the fact that the depositors had the utmost confidence in his word. It was not his money that made people speak well of Peleg P. Akin; it was the worth of the man and the man himself.

Opposite the house of David K. Akin was and is an open field, and at the lower end, near the river, was a public "pound" in which were put stray cattle, but that disappeared years ago, as there were no cattle to put in it, but in those days there were large droves of cows that were driven to different places for pasturage; one place in particular I remember being "old field," formely called "Kelley's Neck," in West Dennis. Every morning a boy collected the cows from different parts of the village and drove them over to that place and every night went for them, always finding the cows patiently waiting at the gate to be driven home.

Before leaving the David K. Akin house I would speak of three negroes who were at one time brought from the South by this old Friend and who for years lived in South Yarmouth. Eli and Noah Morgan and their cousin, Dempsey Ragsdale, were slaves, whom their master wished to set free. (This was of course before the war.) David Akin brought them North and took charge of the two Morgan boys, who were at that time 16 or 18 years of age, while David Kelley took Dempsey, who was nearly white. They all

attended school in the village, made rapid progress in their studies, and at length started out to make their own ways in the world. Dempsey went to sea and from what I can learn, was soon lost to view; Eli became master of a vessel, and Noah went into business in New Bedford, and both became men who were greatly respected wherever they were known. Previous to this, David K. Akin had taken into his house a young colored girl named Lizzie Hill, who was a great favorite with everyone who knew her. She grew up with the other young people and in later life married and went as a missionary to Africa, where she died.

The next house to David K. Akin's was that of Elisha Jenkins. This house was probably built by Cyrenus Kelley, at least it was of him that my father bought it. It is with some hesitation that I write of my father, as my account might be tinged and biased by the deep affection I have for his memory, but in another place I shall take the liberty of inserting one of Mr. Daniel Wing's letters to The Register, that, coming from one outside the family, may be taken for an honest opinion of my father as a man and as a citizen. He was born in West Barnstable, and in his early life worked at his trade in the South, but eventually drifted to South Yarmouth, where he set up the business of shoemaking. He married Mary G. Crowell of West Yarmouth; her two sisters, Sophie and Harriet, married South Yarmouth men, and the three houses or homes were on the same street. In his early days my father was considered an excellent singer; he was always very fond of music, and it is from him that I get my taste for the same art. Both my father and mother were exceedingly fond of reading, which taste was handed down to all of the children.

I have only one story to tell of my father, which I heard from my mother:

One winter's day a man came home with him to stop all night. I do not recall his name, but I think he was one of the many who had worked for my father. Anyway, he was going out to join the Mormons and evidently hoped to secure a convert. He and my father sat up all night discussing and arguing religious questions, while at the same time, the guest was trying to convince his host of the truth of the new doctrine and urging him to leave all, go with him and become a Latter-Day Saint. "And that," said my mother, "is as near as we came to becoming Mormons." Not very near, for I fancy that my father did not get the worst of the argument.

Nearly opposite my father's house was that of Captain Emery

Sears, according to Mr. Wood, which later on became the property of Zeno Baker. Mr. Wood could tell me no particulars of Captain Sears, but I recall Zeno Baker very well. He was a man of excellent education and in winter, when he did not go to sea, he taught school. He taught in the present building, in the old red schoolhouse, in Dennis and other places, and was, for those days, an excellent teacher of the commoner branches. He was also a superior penman and the pages of the secretary's records when he was on the school board are beautifully written.

I remember two stories he used to tell of his experiences as a teacher; one was of a note he received from the parent of one of the pupils, which read:

"ples smiss Mary to recis."

The other was of a boy who had two brothers, Coley and Luke. One day they were all absent, and the next day upon being questioned as to the reason, the boy replied, "Coley, Luke and I, sir, we stayed home from school, sir, 'cause Sally had a sore toe, sir." But why Sally's infirmity should prevent the boys from attending to business I never learned.

It was from a tree in the corner of the lot next to Zeno Baker's that all the so-called "silver leafs" came. I think the original was brought from Maine. We acknowledge they are often a nuisance, but at the same time what would the village have been without them? They are handsome trees, they grow rapidly, they have done much to beautify our streets; we wanted just such a tree, but we did not want so much of them.

Next to Zeno Baker's was the house of George Wing, a brother of Robert and Daniel Wing, senior, now the property of Mrs. Chase. Its appearance then was much like that of its neighbors. At one time it was occupied by Joseph Howland, who came from New Bedford, believing that one could find peace and an absence of temptation in a village of Quakers.

Then came the house of James Davis, recently moved nearer the river and changed beyond recognition of its former self. He had an adopted daughter, Amelia B. Russell; a son, Russell Davis, and a son, William P. Davis, for many years cashier of the First National bank of Yarmouth. Russell Davis was one of those eccentric people who are found in every country village. He was known as "Lord Russ," and stories told of his eccentricities would fill a book. In appearance he was short and thick set, with a merry, laughing face and the rolling gait of a sailor. He was an old bachelor, but

report said that he had had his romance like most others. After the death of his father he built himself a house in the fields near the river, half way between the upper and lower villages. The living room was decorated or papered with pictures cut from magazines and illustrated papers, which were not inartistically arranged or grouped. In one corner of the room was his berth or bunk, similar to those on board ship, for although he had never been to sea, he delighted in everything pertaining to it, and in his leisure hours fashioned some of the most beautiful of miniature ships. He was a great reader; one might say of him that he devoured books, often sitting up all night to finish a story that particularly pleased him. One of his peculiarities was to imagine himself a poet, and as the result, he wrote so called poems without number. Unfortunately, he had no idea of rhyme or rhythm, which at times resulted in making his effusions rather amusing reading. He was always ready to read them at the meetings of the "Lyceum" and they were published in the local papers from time to time, which gratified his pride and really hurt no one.

Across the road from the James Davis house was that of Orlando Baker, which Mr. Wing considers as one of the oldest in the place, 116 years at date of writing. According to Mr. Wing, it was built by Michael Crowell, and conveyed to Benoni Baker and his uncle, Obed Baker, in 1799, the former of whom lived there when he was first married. Michael Crowell was in active business in 1792. He was an uncle of Lewis Crowell and lived in a hollow between Captain Zeno Baker's and the river. He also owned the tract between Main street and the river and between the town landing and a line not far from the old magnesia street. Lewis Crowell lived there before he moved to the "red house." Orlando Baker's garden came across the present street leading to the lower village, for Pleasant street ended at his garden and the street leading to the magnesia factory. His farm sheds were down that street on the other side of his garden. He was one of the original members and a pillar of the Methodist church; a man who lived, to the best of his ability, upright before God and man; more than that none of us can do.

Between the two houses of Orlando Baker and Elisha Jenkins, who by the way, married sisters, was an open piece of land just wide enough for a building and Elisha Taylor of West Yarmouth, who also married a sister, purchased the same and built the house now owned by Captain James L. Whittemore. 'Squire Taylor, as he was called, never did any manual labor in his life; his father

—OLD QUAKER VILLAGE—

left him a little money and by a life of almost penurious saving he accumulated a fair fortune, the income of which supported him and his wife. For many years he was a victim of the "shaking palsy," which affected both his limbs and his speech, so that it was almost impossible for a stranger to understand a word he said. In his younger days he was considered a man of sound judgment and just. He served the town as selectman for twenty-six years, which showed that his townspeople appreciated his worth, or else showed that in those days there was no great desire for office, and considering that there was no money in it and very little glory, it is not to be wondered at that men were kept in office for a quarter of a century. A position of that kind in these days carries with it precious little glory, but the financial reward is by no means small in proportion to the amount of work it entails.

Leading from the Orlando Baker house was a road to the river, and at the foot of it was the magnesia factory, but not in Mr. Wood's boyhood days, for it was not built until 1850. The first factory was burned two years later and then the second structure was erected by its owner, Franklin Fearing. After his death the Wing brothers carried on the business for a time, but the rapid diminishing of the salt works made it impractical to continue it and the building was taken down.

From this point until we come to the place where now stands the summer residence of Freeman C. Goodeno, there were no dwellings, excepting upon the main street. All the land was covered with salt works, which business, as far as South Yarmouth is concerned, must have begun about 1811, according to estimates made by Mr. Wing, although the making of salt by solar evaporation dates back to 1776, and in 1802, according to the reports of the Massachusetts Historical society, over forty thousand bushels of salt were thus made on Cape Cod, several years before South Yarmouth had built its first vat. In 1837, 365,000 bushels of salt were manufactured in the town of Yarmouth valued at $110,000, so that it can be easily seen that when the industry got fairly on its feet it increased rapidly and was a financial success.

From the house of Selim Baker (now Osborne White's) to the house of Hatsel Crosby, there were no houses, but a large area of salt works extended to the river, not to mention many other "stretches" of works farther down, even to the lower village and on the other side of Main street clear to the woods. It was—or rather would be today—a novel sight: those long lines of covered vats containing salt water in various stages of evaporation, while

on the shores were at one time eight mills, whirling and pumping water from the river.

It is a great pity that a few of the salt works and at least one mill could not have been preserved. Few have any idea of the picturesqueness of the river at that time; artists were not long in finding it out and for awhile they were often seen in this region. Then came the era for improving things, and, as is generally the case, the improvements have cost far more than could ever be realized at the time. The actual value of an old mill as a marketable piece of property was not great, but its value in attracting people to the village and in making it something different from other villages was untold. The salt works were a never-failing source of pleasure to the boys; they furnished "slides," to the detriment of one's clothes; they furnished fascinating places to play robbers and pirates; the "coolers" in which salt was handled made splendid canoes, and there were almost a thousand and one entertainments that the salt works and the surroundings furnished.

Having made our tour of the side streets of the village, we come back to the corner of Main and Bridge streets. On the Long pond road, the left hand side going to Yarmouth, was the house of Amos Farris, but on the right hand side there was nothing but pine woods down to the house of David Chubb; then we came to the house of James Covill (later Isaiah), where Sidney Chapman now lives.

Next to it was Reuben Farris's house. He was the miller. It is a low one story house, with a kitchen that goes the whole length of it, and other smaller rooms on the same floor. It was thought in those days that the kitchen was the principal and most important part of the house, and in some respects it is still. Uncle Reuben was a Universalist, and naturally in a community of Friends and Methodists he was not religiously at home, so when the Universalist church was built in South Dennis he attended services there. The next tenant of the house was his son Samuel, who also succeeded him as miller, and later on his grandson, William R., lived there for a number of years.

The next house, that of Mrs. R. D. Farris, was not built until 1856, and the store not until 1866. R. D. Farris was, in the earlier days, a successful merchant. He learned the trade of harness maker of Benjamin Hallett in Yarmouth, the old shop now being next to A. Alden Knowles's store, I believe, and used by Mr. Knowles as a carriage house or barn. His first store or shop was a little building now used by Mrs. Phoebe Farris as a woodhouse.

He gradually added tinware, stoves, etc., and finally groceries. He was naturally a trader, being shrewd and watchful to keep up with the various changes. His first wife was Mercy Easton, and, as he has often told, they went to housekeeping in one room of his father's house. Later on he built the Mrs. Phoebe Farris house and later still the one next to the store.

At the head of Bridge street on Main, was a house occupied by Richard Kelley and later by the Widow Hovey, who kept a boarding house, and later still by William Crocker, Loren Baker and then by Braddock Baker, whose heirs owned it until it was bought by Abiel Howard, torn down and the present house erected. Braddock Baker kept the general store previously run by Baker & Wing. He was a short, heavy man, with stooping shoulders which impressed him firmly in my boyhood mind. He was one of the original members of the Methodist church, and undoubtedly did much to put it on its feet when it was young and struggling. I can remember that both he and his wife were speakers at the prayer meetings, and I also remember that when I was a boy, on being sent to his store in the morning and not finding him in, I would go to his house and generally find him at family prayers. My errand or presence never shortened the service, and I had to wait until the last verse had been read and the last "amen" said. He had several children, among them Darius Baker, judge of the Supreme court of Rhode Island, who at one time was my school teacher. One little thing I remember in connection with the Judge was that one day I took up a volume of Shakespeare which he had been reading, and being too young to know anything of the merits of the great bard, although a book of any kind possessed a fascination for me, I asked if it was "good." He turned to me and said very impressively, "We do not speak of Shakespeare as 'good'; it is very interesting." That was a lesson for me, and I never forgot it.

In the late Mrs. Delyra Wood's house lived William Farris, father of Allen Farris, who lived farther down the street. His wife, Aunt Liddy, was a large woman, a good, motherly soul, who was one of the greatest talkers I have ever known. She would come over to my mother's house as far as the door, in too much of a hurry to come in, and there she would stand and talk for half or three-quarters of an hour. Her daughter, also named Liddy, and wife of Zeno Baker, was one of the smartest women to work and one of the kindest of neighbors. I shall never forget Aunt Liddy Baker, for she spanked me for stealing her pears, and strange to say, my

mother whipped me for the same offense when I got home!

The present Methodist church is but little over sixty years old, so that we can hardly speak of it as "old." It was not standing when Mr. Wood was a boy, and was built after I was born, so we will simply say it is growing old.

But in the yard or enclosure leading to the present schoolhouse there was a building, "the little red schoolhouse," the old district schoolhouse, which now stands back of the bank and is used as a storehouse. Here Mr. Wood went to school; here Mr. Wing went to school, to Zeno Baker as teacher. Mr. Wood remembers David Kelley as his teacher at one time, and Sophia Crocker of West Barnstable. The curriculum was not extended, but the "three Rs" were well taught and the ground work well laid for a higher education if the pupil was ambitious to go farther than the district school could take him. Spelling schools and spelling contests were popular in those days, and the old schoolhouse witnessed many an exciting time in such diversions.

The present schoolhouse, built in 1855, ended the usefulness of the old building, which was removed to another location and used for more ignoble purposes. The marks of the seats, the depressions in the floor, the names written on the plastering, are still there. The fiftieth anniversary of the opening of the present schoolhouse took place in June, 1905, and was participated in by all the pupils of the public schools of the town.

The house of Zenas Wood, in which his son, Orlando Wood, lived during the last years of his life, stood next to the schoolhouse grounds, and was built by Moses Burgess. He came from West Barnstable, worked at his trade, that of a carpenter, and built for himself this house. Later, he moved back to his old home. Orlando F. Wood was a notable example of a young old-man. He was born in the village in 1825 in a house that stood upon the spot now occupied by the paint shop of Manton H. Crowell. As a boy he attended school in the little old red schoolhouse which stood on the present school grounds, at the little Friends' schoolhouse which stood on land of the late David K. Akin, between his house and that now occupied by Frank L. Baker, and at the "academy." He went to sea when a boy, the principal incident of which was that he fell from aloft and narrowly escaped death. He worked in the "rope-walk" and later learned the tailor's trade in South Yarmouth, which trade he practised in New Bedford and Boston, eventually returning to his native village, where he lived until his death in 1911, at the age of 86.

Next to the Zenas Wood house stood the shoe shop of Elisha Jenkins, my father, and it is to Mr. Wing that I am indebted for the following, which was published in the Yarmouth Register:

"The shoe store now owned and occupied by Mr. E. T. Baker and situated on Main street, is an enlargement of the long, low building where, some years ago, shoes were both made and sold. At one time a number of young shoemakers from Lynn were employed there. They were full of fun and frolic, and in those days of practical jokes, if a neighbor's horse was found in the morning, gaily striped with bright colors, or if some sailor man was unable to open any of his outwardly swinging doors because of a chain cable passed entirely around his house and attached to an anchor set deep in the lot on the opposite side of the street, the mischief was quite likely to be charged to the shoe-shop employes.

"So far back, however, as the memory of the writer reaches, Elisha Jenkins was the proprietor and sole occupant. A man of more than ordinary intellectual power, a deep thinker, possessed of a wonderful memory, a reader of good books, a lover of history, intensely patriotic, fond of young people, instructive in conversation, the writer will always feel indebted to him for the pleasure of many an hour spent in his company. All through the Civil war, when news of more than ordinary interest was expected, the arrival of the evening mail would almost invariably find an attractive audience assembled at his shop, listening with breathless interest as some one read aloud the latest news from the seat of war.

"I can see now the rack of lasts at one end of the room, with a wooden bench in front of it; cases of boots (long-legged ones) standing here and there; the cobbler's bench of the proprietor in the southwest corner, with its depressed seat and its square compartments for wooden pegs, iron nails, shoemaker's wax, bundles of bristles, and its usual assortment of awls, hammers, etc., while the drawer beneath contained pieces of leather and supplies of sundry sorts.

"The Thanksgiving proclamation of Governor George N. Briggs with 'God save the Commonwealth of Massachusetts' in bold type at the bottom, hung on the south wall for years and seemed to become one of the fixtures of the place. The wooden post in the centre of the room, close by the wood burning stove, was used when a customer came in and ordered a new pair of boots or shoes to be made expressly for him. With his heel against the post,

the length of the foot was marked on the floor with a knife. Close by was the tub of water in which the pieces of leather were soaked to make them pliable. The north room contained a stock of boots, shoes and rubbers, mostly arranged upon shelves on two of the side walls. Congress boots were unknown to the earlier times, and as a boy, the writer can remember with what pleasure he went there each autumn to be fitted to a pair of long-legged boots, having square patches of red morocco at the top in front, and with a stout strap on either side of each. No costlier pair since has ever quite equalled in splendor those specimens of long ago. Such were some of the attractions for a boy; the features which in later years made deepest impressions upon the memory were the conversations with the genial proprietor."

Ebenezer Hallett's house and tannery stood on the spot where now stands the house of Reuben K. Farris. It was a low, double house, and back of it was a tannery. Later on, Leonard Underwood, a Friend, purchased it and the tannery was discontinued. He was a carpenter and lived there but a few years, moving to Fall River. When the house was torn down Allen Farris built the large double house still standing.

There was nothing in the way of buildings until we came to "Mill lane." The Isaiah Homer house had not at that time been moved from Yarmouth, but there were two houses on the northeasterly side of the lane. One of these was occupied by Samuel Eaton Kelley, and was afterwards moved to the corner of Main street, and is now the home of Captain Alonzo Kelley; the other is still standing and was occupied by James Covill and others.

Isaiah Homer moved from Yarmouth and was one of our most respected of citizens. He had a little shoe shop in one corner of his yard on Main street and there he worked for years. He was a man who, even in his old age, showed remarkable powers of physical endurance and I have often watched him with admiration as he walked off as smartly and lightly as would a much younger man; there was no sign of physical decrepitude. He was born on the North side in an old house that was undoubtedly the first church built in Yarmouth, that is, the framework was the same if nothing else; it is known now as the "Hannah Crowell house" and is one of the historical relics on the north side of the town. The family possesses many old relics of the Homer family, but none of them more curious than a bill of sale of a negro, dated Feb. 20, 1776. In it F. W. Homer acknowledges receiving from his father, Benjamin Homer, forty pounds for two-thirds of a negro named

"Forten." According to the late Charles F. Swift, "Forten" lived to see his race declared free.

On the opposite side of Mill lane, on the corner, lived Josiah Baker, James Lewis, "Uncle Levi" and others. Of these and their families I have nothing to say.

The old grist mill that stood at the head of the lane was run in Mr. Wood's early days by Reuben Farris and in my early days by Samuel Farris, his son, and by Romegio Lewis. It was originally on the north side of the Cape and was moved to its present location in 1782. The people of South Yarmouth made a great mistake when they allowed it to be sold and taken from the village. It is now in West Yarmouth on the land of the late Mr. Abell and attracts much attention from visitors from all parts of the country. A similar mill stands in the lower village.

Coming to the house now occupied by Ernest P. Baker, Mr. Wood said, "In my day old Cato, a negro, had a small house on that lot, in which he lived with his daughter. His wife was a fullblooded Indian, and at one time they had a wigwam on the land which was the garden of David K. Akin, and next to the house of Elisha Jenkins." Alden, in his "Memorabilia of Yarmouth," speaks of old Cato as living in a wigwam there in 1797, and he also says that in 1779 there was a small cluster of wigwams about a mile from the mouth of Bass river. According to Mr. Wing, Cato was living in 1831.

Daniel Weaver's house (now Mrs. Matilda Smith's), was then standing. He was a weaver by name and by trade, and wove carpets, probably the once favorite rag carpet. I thought it was he, but have since been corrected, who invented a perpetual motion machine, which he exhibited to a select company in the academy. The company assembled, the machine was produced, but somehow it refused to work; the exhibition was a failure and the machine went the way of thousands of similar inventions.

I do not know how old the Heman Crowell house is, which when Mr. Wing was a boy was occupied by Minerva Crowell, who had three children; Laban Baker owned the other half of the house.

The Frank Homer house was occupied by John Cannon and by Venny Crowell, grandfather of the late Mrs. Henry Taylor. It is related that it was here that his son, Venny Crowell, met his wife. She was passing through the village and stopped to get a glass of water; the son saw her, and afterwards married her. Both father and son were tall, spare men of rugged frames and great endurance. Once upon a time, at a revival meeting, one of the

women exhorters and singers asked Uncle Venny if he did not like music? He was honest, and replied that he liked singing but he hated to hear it murdered!

In the present house of Mrs. Albert White, although now much changed of course, lived Dr. Apollos Pratt, an eccentric old country practitioner. The stories told of the old man are without number, many of them very amusing. He had two daughters; one became the wife of Captain Seleck H. Matthews, and the other the wife of Freeman Matthews. The doctor was given to telling wonderful yarns; among others, he told of a patient of his who had been given up as incurable, but he disemboweled him, killed a sheep and substituted the intestines, and the man got well. On being asked how it seemed to affect the man afterwards, he said, in no way particularly, except that "he had a h——l of a hankering for grass!" One evening while talking with one of his familiars, they agreed to see who could tell the biggest lie. The other man said he could see the man in the moon. "Well," said the doctor, as he gazed earnestly at the sky, "I can see him wink;" which certainly required the better eyesight. Mr. Wood said he had frequently seen the old man sitting in a rocking chair by the window, the floor being worn in ridges where he had rocked back and forth, year after year. He died in 1860, aged 83 years.

On a short street in the vicinity of the present Standish hall was a little house belonging to Ormond Easton, which was later moved to the river opposite the magnesia factory, and was known as the "Noah Morgan house."

There was no house from Dr. Pratt's to that of Barnabas Sears, the space being filled with salt works. The Isaiah Crocker house was not built then nor was that of David Sears.

The Barnabas Sears house, according to Mr. Wing, originally stood in a field near James pond and was built by Ebenezer Baker. It was moved to its present location in 1753 by John Kelley, senior. This is the second oldest house in the village; its curved rafters, low eves and ancient appearance make it an object of great interest to visitors. Barnabas Sears had five sons: Seth, who died while a young man, John, Stephen, Barnabas and David, all of whom lived near the old homestead, and for years his daughter, Elizabeth Stetson, lived in the house. Aunt Lizzie, as she was called, was the last of the Quaker preachers of the South Yarmouth meeting, and to hear her prayers brought me as near the throne of God as I ever expect to be in this world. Her words were earnest and simple, but her very earnestness, and her

firm belief that her words were heard by the Father, impressed me greatly. She was a large woman, and tall, almost masculine in many ways, and when she was a girl it is said that she was equal to any man in riding a horse or managing one. Of her the following story is told:

When she was a young woman, she was riding through the woods one day when she came upon a minister leading his horse from the blacksmith's. "Why don't thee ride thy horse instead of leading him?" she asked. "Because," said the minister, "he won't allow me to put the bridle over his head, and he bites and kicks so I am afraid of him." "Give it to me," she said, with a look of contempt at his ignorance, and jumping from her horse she whipped off her apron and flinging it over the horse's head deftly adjusted the bridle. "There, friend, a little brains used intelligently may be useful in other ways than in writing sermons," she said. "True," replied the minister, "but unfortunately, I do not wear aprons."

Although the houses of the sons of Barnabas Sears were not in existence seventy-five years ago, they were men who were looked up to in the community. Barnabas, Jr., and John K. were carpenters and builders, and at one time they had a steam sawmill back of their house near the woods, called the "Pawkunnawkut mill." Stephen was for many years a teacher, and served the town as selectman and as school committee. David, "Uncle David" as most of us called him, was one of the most genial souls among us and needs no words of introduction to those for whom these pages are written.

The next house from Barnabas Sears, senior, was that now occupied by Charles I. Gill, who purchased it from the estate of Reuben J. Baker. Mr Baker, familiarly known as "Blind Reuben" because of his loss of eyesight when a boy, was the son of Captain Reuben Baker, whose wife, Louisa, afterwards married William Gray. In many respects he was a remarkable man, for in spite of his blindness he carried on a successful grocery business for years.

Next to this house was that of Captain Freeman Baker. Mr. Wing says that opposite this house, in the middle of the main road, was a house belonging to the Widow Marchant, the travelled roadway passing on either side.

The Baptist church was then standing, but it bore no resemblance to the church of today. It stood with its eaves to the street and had no belfry or steeple. It bore no evidence of paint

without and was very plain within, as plain as the Friends meeting house. Aunt Lizzie Stetson named it "The Lord's barn." Mr. Wing has this to say of it:

"At times there was no regular service there, but the young people of the village nearby could count with a certainty upon the annual temperance meeting as long as Barnabas Sears, senior, was living, for his interest in the temperance cause was deep and abiding, as indeed it was in the religious society of which he was a devoted member. Either side of each aisle was a row of old-fashioned pews with high backs. The pulpit was a long, box-like affair, some two and a half or three feet above the floor level, with steps leading up to it on its righthand corner. A door at the head of the steps kept out those not eligible to that enclosure, and a seat along the front of the pulpit was known as the "deacon's seat." The pews at the lefthand side of the pulpit faced the front of the building, while those in the opposite corner faced the pulpit. A lot of lighted tallow candles placed in different parts of the room did their best to overcome the natural darkness of the place, and when with blackened wicks hanging to one side they seemed ready to give up the task, the ever-watchful Father Sears, even then an old man, would go around with a candle snuffer and carefully remove the charred portions of the wicks and so brighten up the place until his services in that line were again needed.

"Father Sears was a thoughtful, earnest man, highly respected by both old and young, and although his quaint language would provoke a smile, it was not a token of disrespect, but often of pleasure, caused by the reviving of features that all realized were rapidly passing away. On one occasion, when some of the smaller portion of the audience became somewhat restless and began to leave the room, Mr. Sears stopped the exercises and in his usually dignified manner said, "All those who want for to go out will go out, and all those who want for to stay in will stay in." I think there was no more passing out until the close of the meeting, and the quaint language and impressive manner remain in my memory as a pleasing feature of the occasion.

"The Baptist church in South Yarmouth was organized in 1824. The structure itself dates back to the year 1826, when it was built at a cost of $600, the whole amount being paid by Rev. Simeon Crowell and Captain Freeman Baker, the former being the first pastor there."

In 1860 extensive alterations were made in it, and in 1891 it was again remodeled and put in its present shape. Mr Wood spoke of

the church as "Uncle Sim's church," and says that he attended Sunday school there and that Lurania Lewis was his teacher.

He also attended Sunday school at the old Methodist meeting house which stood farther up the road towards West Yarmouth, and of which the only present reminder is the cemetery. This church, which Mr. Wood calls "Uncle Siley's church," was built by Silas Baker, senior, who came from Harwich. He died in 1844, aged 78 years. In a measure, Uncle Siley ran the church to suit himself during his life, as, having built it, he thought he had the right to do. The Rev. Mr. Winchester was the preacher and Elisha Parker was Mr. Wood's Sunday school teacher. The worshippers who came from any distance brought their luncheons and made it an all-day duty. On one occasion Mr. Wood had his lunch stolen from the pew, which awful crime he remembered all his life, for he had to go hungry. The choir was in the long gallery at the back of the church, and a big bass viol was the accompaniment for the singers.

There were two little schoolhouses a little way below or beyond the church; one of them near the residence of Jerry Eldridge, the other I cannot place, but they were not more than a hundred yards apart.

Returning up Main street on the opposite side, Mr. Wood said there were no houses until we got to that of Mrs. Cyrus White, formerly occupied by her father, Captain Barnabas Eldridge, who died in 1846, aged 46 years, and then a long strip of field land until we came to the little old house that was always known as "the old maids'." The occupants of the house were known as "the three old maids" although two of them had been married. Robert Homer married one of them after a courtship of forty years, and it is said that he remarked that he wished he had courted forty years longer. These old ladies had very amusing ways and were the victims of many practical jokes at the hands of ungodly boys. On one occasion they were routed out of bed in the middle of the night by some young men who asked if they had seen a red and white cow pass that way. They had not, and the young men were advised to go over to "Brother Freeman's and ask him." The young men retired, the door was shut and the old ladies presumably had returned to their beds, when again came loud rappings at the door; another procession from the bedrooms, and there stood the same young men, who said that they thought they would come back and tell them that "Brother Freeman" had not seen the cow! I have thought it a great pity that those old ladies could not

have sought comfort in a few swear words. When the last of this trio died, the contents of the house were sold at auction and among other things an old bureau, in the lining of which the purchaser found a $100 check which proved to be good and was collected.

The present building of Mrs. Sturgess Crowell was then standing, occupied by Captain Elisha Baker, as was the house occupied by Elisha T. Baker. Of the latter, Mr. Wood said that he remembered that Solomon Crowell had a little dry goods store in one of the front rooms; later it became the property of Mrs. Baker's father, Captain Frederick White.

Then we come to the old house known as "Major Dimmick's," formerly owned by Major D. Baker, "Major" being his name and not his title as one might infer. Old Uncle Amos Baker lived there, but what relation he was to Major I do not know.

The house of Peter Goodnow was not standing, but his father had a house by the river exactly upon the spot where is now the summer residence of his grandson, Freeman C. Goodnow.

The Hatsel Crosby house was built with the front door on the side, the carpenter, Job Otis of New Bedford, who drew the plans, having the idea that Main street ran north and south ordered the front door on the south side, supposing that it really would be facing Main street and upon the front side of the house. It was built by Uncle Russell Davis, who lived there with his wife Phoebe. He was a brother of James Davis, and a Quaker preacher. Hatsel Crosby came from Brewster and went into the salt making business. He married several times and had a large family of children, none of whom, however, live in South Yarmouth. He died in 1896, aged 89 years.

From this point to the house of Selim Baker the section was given up to salt works, and all of the houses on this side of the street are comparatively new. Selim Baker's house was built some years before the salt works were taken down. He was a carpenter by trade, a man prominent in church affairs and much respected. His daughter, Mrs. Osborne White, lives in the house, which has been greatly changed.

The Academy came next; it sat well back from the street. It had a belfry and a bell—the only school building in South Yarmouth that ever did—and was quite an imposing looking structure. It was built in 1844 and owned by the citizens of the place, and was used as a private school, the idea of its promoters being to furnish better educational facilities for their children than could be found at the district school. That its reputation during its

short career was high was shown by the fact that a large number of pupils came from away. It ceased to exist as a school when the present public schoolhouse was opened in 1855, and was converted into a dwelling house in 1862, after having been moved close to the street, by the father of the present Zenas P. Howes. Mr. Alonzo Tripp was the first teacher, and Mr. Adams the last.

The house formerly belonging to Mrs. Elisha Parker and now to the heirs of Benjamin Homer, was built by William P. Davis, but he did not live in it many years for he accepted a position in the Yarmouth National bank and was cashier of that institution from 1875 to 1895. He also was town treasurer for over fifty years. Elisha Parker, who bought the house of him, was then living in the lower village. He was at one time in the shoe business, and later during the Civil war was very successful in the wool business.

The next house was that of Aunt Mima Wood, which stood near the spot where now stands the house formerly occupied by Dr. E. M. Parker. She was the widow of Tilson Wood, and her son David used to wheel her to Friends meeting in a wheelbarrow; she died in 1841. Frank Wood built the present house. He was a stone mason, and did the stone work on the abutments of the Bass river bridge, and split the stone for the foundations of his own house from boulders on Town Hills. He died in 1853, aged 56.

We now come to the place from which we started, the corner of Main and Bridge street. The house on the corner was built in 1831 by Abiel Akin for his son Joseph, who was a brother of David K., and like him interested in salt making. Joseph Akin had three children, Catherine, Frederick and Charles, the last of whom only is living. Catherine Akin was a remarkable woman in many respects and especially in the ambition she possessed and in the power of will that enabled her to fit herself for a position in the world which she occupied. When hardly more than a girl she began to teach in the little district school in Georgetown, studying nights to keep ahead of her classes. Later she was the principal of a boarding school which became famous as "Miss Akin's school" in Stamford, Conn. Throughout her life her friends remained loyal to her and her pupils loved her and became her friends. She was always very fond of her native village, and it is in the old Quaker cemetery, within sight of the river she loved, and where the ever murmuring pines sing a requiem, that she sleeps.

QUAINT STORIES.

One old Quaker forbade his son to go upon the ice, but in coming from school they passed the pond, and his companion, venturing upon the ice, fell through and would have been drowned but for the aid of the boy who had been forbidden to go. He did not dare to tell his father about it for fear of the consequences, but the old gentleman heard of it, and while commending his son for saving his companion's life he thrashed him soundly for disobedience.

The old Quakers were averse to worldly music; to them it was one of the snares of the evil one. It is related that one of them beat his son soundly for playing upon a jews-harp, and when some of the apprentices in a neighboring shoe shop got possession of a fife and drum he closed all the windows and doors to keep out the sinful sounds.

Another good old Quaker lady was so worked up over the singing of hymns at the Methodist church, which she could hear from her house, that she declared she "had rather hear it thunder."

Two young men who did not possess as much of the Quaker sanctity as they should, considering their bringing up, but who did possess a deal of worldly desires, shut themselves up in an old salthouse and while one played on an old flute the other danced a breakdown. Then they came forth, feeling that for once they had been like other fellows and thoroughly wicked!

The late Catherine Akin used to delight in telling the following story, and although it loses much of the real humor it possessed when told by herself, for she was an inimitable story teller, it will give one an idea of the strictness of those early Friends.

It seems that Miss Akin had a piano in her father's house, an innovation looked upon with a great deal of disfavor by the old Quakers, and while they did not openly make objections, it was known that they thoroughly disapproved of it. Miss Akin's mother had a gathering of the Friends to tea, and on that occasion it was thought best to close the piano, so that even the sight of it might not cause offense; its cover was put on and books and other things

arranged so that it would not be too noticeable. In the evening someone, probably more worldly minded, asked Miss Akin to play something, which she of course declined, evidently having been coached by her parents, and her father said that perhaps the others would not approve of it. "Well," said Aunt Ruth, after a pause, "thee might play something if thee played it very slow." What she played, whether it was a quick-step in the time of "Old Hundred" or the "Dead March" from "Saul" I do not know, but it evidently gave satisfaction. Someone told Miss Akin that they saw Uncle Silas and Aunt Ruth, at another time, standing by the window while she was playing, but what they thought of it she never knew.

As in all country villages, occasionally there has been one whose mind has given away, and years ago there was a man who went insane upon religion. One of the pleasures of the boys in the country is the ringing of the bells the night before the Fourth of July, being unable to restrain their patriotic feelings longer than the last stroke of the bell at midnight. One night they had stolen into the Methodist church, made their way up the dark stairs and begun to ring the bell, when in walked the aforesaid "crazy man" carrying a long butcher's knife with which he threatened the boys. He told them to kneel down while he prayed, and said that if they attempted to leave he would cut their ears off. And there he kept them for hours, kneeling in fear and trembling, while he prayed for them, knife in hand, glancing about from time to time to see that the boys were properly devout and attentive. It was the most quiet "night before the Fourth" that had been known for several years, for the boys were in no mood to continue the bell ringing when the last "amen" was said and they were released.

THE BREAKWATER.

Quoting again from Mr. Wing:
"The breakwater was built about the year 1837 from material which came mostly from Dinah's pond. A continual hawser of about four and a half inch size was stretched from the mouth of the river to the breakwater site and by its help the scows were pulled to and fro. This undertaking proved a failure on account of the formation of sand bars on the in-shore side.

"Work was suspended and the structure has never been completed according to the original plans. A wooden building which

was erected upon the central portion of the breakwater was set on fire and destroyed by sailors some years ago.

"According to tradition both the old pier and the breakwater have received great quantities of smuggled goods in the years of long ago.

"During the war of 1812-15 some of the smaller vessels of the English fleet visited this part of the coast and demanded a thousand dollars as tribute money. A committee endeavored to raise the money by subscription and at last succeeded in securing the whole of the amount required. This they sent to the English in two installments by a citizen known as "Uncle Abner." The object of the business portion of the community was to impress upon the minds of the enemy that none but poor ignorant fishermen dwelt thereabouts, in order that they might escape the requisition of a larger sum. The messenger was well chosen, and an address was sent to the "Commander of the British Squadron on the coast of Boston Bay" etc. On returning to shore the messenger stated that he had been kindly received; was taken to the cabin and that he not only delivered the written address but spoke to some length to the assembled officers, who listened respectfully, evidently much moved by his words of pleading for the poor fishermen. Before leaving, the British agreed not to molest any fishing vessel that could show a license from Uncle Abner. The English kept their word and vessels having the requisite permit from Uncle Abner were not disturbed."

OLD PIER.

The following extract from the "Collection of the Massachusetts Historical society," Vol. VIII, which is headed "A Description of Dennis in the County of Barnstable. September, 1802," has been handed to me by Mr. Freeman C. Goodnow, a former resident of the village and at the present time the owner of a summer cottage here, will be found of interest as it gives a good description of the old pier as it was in 1802, and judging from it we should infer that the pier was built in the vicinity of 1800.

"Half way between the river's mouth and the end of the bar, stands a pier 37 feet long and 31 feet broad, on which is a store. There is good anchorage 2 cables length east of it and 12 feet of water at low tide. Common tides rise here 4 feet. Such is Bass river. The harbor which it affords might be improved by art. Mr. Sylvanus Crowell, who lives in Yarmouth and who built the

pier, has endeavored to confine the water of the river within the main channel and to prevent it flowing through the marsh on the eastern side, but his laudable attempts have hitherto failed of success. Persevering labors may perhaps, in time, effect the wished for object."

When the old pier disappeared I do not know, but the irregular piles of rock were a guide to those entering the river, for if the rocks could not be seen then there was sufficient water to enter. During the War of 1812 it must have been a busy place, vessels discharging cargoes, fishermen taking in salt, and purchasing supplies.

From this same article quoted above:

"On the Yarmouth side (of Bass river) there are six wharfs, three near the mouth of the river and three north of it. There are here twenty-one vessels, one brig sails immediately for the West Indies, ten coasters from 30 to 40 tons burden sail to Boston, Connecticut or the Southern states and thence to the West Indies. The other ten vessels are fishermen, one of a hundred tons, the rest are smaller. The fishing vessels go to the Straits of Belle Isle, the shoals of Nova Scotia or Nantucket sound. On a medium, a fishing vessel uses 700 bushels of salt in a year. One or two vessels are annually built in Bass river, chiefly on the western side."

The article closes with these words:

"These facts in addition to those which have been made already, and which will hereafter be mentioned in this volume, show the present flourishing state of the South shore of the county of Barnstable, a part of Massachusetts not often visited and little known."

FIFTIETH ANNIVERSARY
of the
Methodist Episcopal Church.
Sept. 3 and 4, 1902.

The exercises began on the evening of Sept. 3 with a social gathering of welcome to the visitors and the friends of the society. The pastor at this time was Rev. A. J. Jolly, who made the opening address of welcome. Addresses were made by several of the former pastors, and letters read from many who were unable to be present. Members of the choir and others furnished enjoyable music.

The celebration was continued on Wednesday afternoon, and in the evening there was a religious service at which the Rev. L. B. Bates, D. D., preached the sermon, music being furnished by members of the choir in former days.

FIFTIETH ANNIVERSARY
of the Erection of the Present School Buildings.
June 9, 1905.

The celebration took place in Lyceum hall, Yarmouthport, in the afternoon, and all the children of the schools were present and took part in the exercises. The speakers were Mr. George H. Cary of Boston and Mr. Stephen Sears of South Yarmouth. Prayer was offered by the Rev. Arthur Varley, Mr. E. W. Eldridge presided, Mr. W. A. Schwab gave the address of welcome, and an original poem, of which the following is a part, was read by Mr. E. Lawrence Jenkins:

The Old School Buildings.

Fifty years the staunch old buildings
 Weathered have the rain and snow;
Stood amid the storm and sunshine,
 Watched the seasons come and go.

Fifty years within those class rooms,
 Children have been taught to climb
Up the grand old path of knowledge,
 Leading to the heights sublime.

Fifty years of grand, brave service,
 Teaching thousands ow to live;
Storing in their minds the knowledge
 That to others they might give.

Fifty years have seen the passing
 From their portals to the world,
Thousands of young men and maidens,
 With their banners bright unfurled.

And they stand today, those buildings,
 Just as strong and true as then;
They were builded upon honor,
 They were built by honest men.

And a thought it is most pleasant,
 They were builded thus to last,

E'en as character was builded
 By those pupils in the past.
    *   *   *   *
Fifty years have others labored
 At the tasks now set for you;
Many more will follow after,
 Many more these tasks will do.

May you then strive in the doing
 Just the very best you can;
Study hard, each day improving,
 Each for each, as man for man.
    *   *   *   *
Honor to those staunch old buildings,
 Honor for the work they've done
For our fathers and our mothers,
 And their children, every one.

The anniversary hymn was written by Mr. E. F. Pierce, principal of the high school.

FIFTY YEARS AGO.
Tune: "Fair Harvard."

Far, far through the mists of the hurrying years,
 Away to those days ever dear,
Fond memory guides us and sings to our ears
 Of that work, sure, far-seeing and clear.
And shall we forget in this circle so bright,
 Those builders of fifty years gone?
With steadfastness, foresight, with eyes toward the light,
 They builded for children unborn.

We breathe the same air of the murmuring seas;
 We tread paths that their footsteps have worn;
These loved scenes, this dear schoolhouse, these whispering trees,
 Speak to us, as to them, of life's dawn.
So, while onward we press, life's full duties to meet,
 Wheresoever our lot may be cast,
We remember in honor, in gratitude sweet,
 The brave work of the men of the past.

—OLD QUAKER VILLAGE— 49

The following interesting article has been received from Mr. Daniel Wing which gives valuable information.

THE FRIENDS' BURIAL GROUNDS IN YARMOUTH.

About the year 1714 there stood on the highway a short distance north of Kelley's bay in what is now a part of Dennis, but was then within the boundaries of Yarmouth, a small building owned and occupied by the Society of Friends or Quakers as a meeting house.

For about a century, possibly more, the meetings there were attended by members coming from various directions; some of them from sections quite distant from the place of worship; and there is yet an old roadway in that vicinity known to the older generation as "the Quaker path."

With the opening up of the Indian reservation in South Yarmouth for settlement by whites, the centres of population were affected somewhat, and the present Friends' meeting house was built in 1809 for the better accommodation of the generation of that time.

In accordance with the custom prevailing in those days, the burial place was located in each case upon the grounds adjacent to the place for worship.

In 1875 the grounds of the old site were surrounded by a neat wooden fence; but in 1901 the writer received a letter saying, "Alas! the fence has fallen; who will restore it?" In 1903 a new wooden fence was built, enclosing, however, only that portion of the grounds which had been used for burial purposes.

And now the question forcibly presents itself: Who will, in the coming years, see that this ancient cemetery is properly cared for and protected?

For many years the grounds of the South Yarmouth meeting house were enclosed by a wooden fence; but this was eventually replaced by a more durable construction of stone and iron.

The earlier Friends nowhere showed their traits of modesty and simplicity more prominently than in their meeting houses and burial grounds. The former were marked examples of architectural simplicity and the latter showed a complete abstinence from ostentation and vain glory.

To these early Friends, Death leveled all human distinctions, and in the grave, sinner and saint rested alike so far as outward manifestations were concerned. A simple mound of earth marked the

last resting place, and no tablet was allowed to distinguish one burial from another.

Years passed, and a rule was adopted allowing the placing of headstones not exceeding eighteen inches in height, with simple inscription showing name and age. This occurred not far from the middle of the last century. Today although

> "No storied urn nor animated bust
> In grandeur stands above their silent dust,
> The lowly headstones, standing row on row,
> Reveal to us all that we need to know."

From the earliest days, this place of burial, although owned and controlled by Friends, has been essentially a village cemetery. Of the first thirty-one adult burials there, less than one-half were members of the Friends' society, and when the number of burials reached two hundred and sixty-six, less than one-third were members by birthright or otherwise.

The privilege thus extended to persons not connected with them by ties of religious belief, shows great neighborliness of feeling and emphasizes the thought so prominent in the minds of the early Friends, that at the grave human judgment should end, and that the merits or demerits of the deceased should be left to God, who judgeth not as man judgeth.

Each succeeding year the membership grows perceptibly less, and to one who remembers events connected with those honored people of the past during a period of nearly seventy years, a review of the former days brings a feeling of deep sadness.

> It seems but yesterday those scenes were laid,
> And yet it needs no prophet's wondrous aid
> To show us that those goodly scenes of yore
> Have long since passed and will return no more.

Maywood, Ill., 1915.   Daniel Wing.

And now we come to the last words.

The editor confesses that there is much more that might be said; there are many names that might claim a place within these pages,—men who were an active part of the building up of the village, and who occupied positions that entitle them to the remembrance of the public, but the plan of these reminiscences is to picture the earlier aspect of Quaker village, rather than to form a series of biographies, although the editor confesses that at times he has been led away from the original idea. He also is well aware that more information could have been procured if he had known where to apply for it, but a public appeal through the Yarmouth Register failed of responses except in one instance. He has done what he could, only regretting that much that is of value and interest must, in the course of years, be hopelessly lost. The errors that may occur in any of the statements are such that could only come from incorrect information; the editor has presented it as given to him by various people, as they have heard it or it has been handed down to them.

1973

Milton Keynes UK
Ingram Content Group UK Ltd.
UKHW050741261023
431328UK00015B/300